# Four Faces of Authority

Discovering Your Authority Avatar

Brian Horn & Jack Mize

FOUR FACES OF AUTHORITY

Copyright © 2014 Authority Media Group, LLC

All rights reserved. No portion of this book may be reproduced--mechanically, electronically, or by any other means without the expressed written permission of the authors except as provided by the United States of America copyright law.

Published by Authority Media Group, LLC Houston, TX

ISBN: 978-1499350890

The Publisher has strived to be as accurate and complete as possible in the creation of this book.

This book is not intended for use as a source of legal, business, accounting or financial advice. All readers are advised to seek services of competent professionals in legal, business, accounting, and finance field.

In practical advice books, like anything else in life, there are no guarantees of income made. Readers are cautioned to rely on their own judgment about their individual circumstances to act accordingly.

While all attempts have been made to verify information provided in this publication, the Publisher assumes no responsibility for errors, omissions, or contrary interpretation of the subject matter herein. Any perceived slights of specific persons, peoples, or organizations are unintentional.

# CONTENTS

| | |
|---|---|
| WHAT IS AUTHORITY POSITIONING? | 1 |
| WHAT MAKES ME AN AUTHORITY? | 9 |
| THE AUTHORITY MINDSET | 17 |
| THE FOUR FACES – YOUR AUTHORITY AVATAR | 25 |
| JOE EVERYMAN | 29 |
| THE COWBOY | 35 |
| THE SOLDIER | 39 |
| THE WIZARD | 43 |
| WHICH AUTHORITY ARE YOU? | 47 |
| DON'T TRY AND PLEASE EVERYONE | 53 |
| CLAIMING YOUR AUTHORITY | 57 |
| GARRET J WHITE ON AUTHORITY ALCHEMY | 65 |

# WHAT IS AUTHORITY POSITIONING?

*"When you're small, you need to appear big"*

**General Sun Tzu – The Art of War**

In The Art of War, the famous General Sun Tzu said that "When you're small, you need to appear big." Although he probably didn't mean for this simple statement to be marketing advice, it is, indeed, an incredibly important point to remember, as entrepreneurs, when positioning yourself as an authority in your industry.

So what exactly is an authority when it comes to business? To some it's synonymous with being the expert, thought leader, perhaps guru of an industry.

Many think expert or authority status can only be attained by convincing enough people that they are smarter than anyone else in their field.

Well, they'd be wrong. In fact, what most people consider to be the path to expert status and authority positioning is just unrealistic and as difficult as hunting a unicorn

So let's get very clear and start with what Authority is NOT.

We want to bust the top 5 myths that we've found so many entrepreneurs believe are what it takes to be a recognized authority.

# Myth #1 - To be an expert you just need to call yourself an expert.

This has been a popular thought for many, many years in the marketing world. Frankly, it's nothing more than an easy answer to a complex question that's consistently taught to salespeople and entrepreneurs. While it may have been mildly effective in the past, it's not how you see most industry leaders achieve their success and reach real authority status.

It goes far beyond that. You can't simply just call yourself an expert any more and expect the masses to take you at your word. However, you can easily be the person that takes the actions that will make it easy for others to call you the expert.

That's what real authority is. Having others recognize you as the expert, and it's easier than most make it out to be.

## Myth #2 - An expert is a person that knows everything about their industry and subject matter.

Well, the fact is, that person just doesn't exist. No one knows everything there is about his or her industry, and those that claim they do actually diminish their credibility because people know it's just not possible.

An expert is someone that knows enough to be able to help their customers and their prospects and they also have to be willing to share that knowledge.

# Myth #3 - An expert is the very best at what they do in their field.

You can probably think of someone right now, who's considered an expert or an authority in your industry, whether it's fitness, marketing, financial, or real estate. Go ahead, get that person in your mind. Now ask yourself, "Does this person really know any more than I do? Are they the best at what they do?"

So why are they considered the authority? More importantly, why aren't you?

# Myth # 4 - It takes years to build expert reputation so that credible media will recognize you as an authority.

Well, that's the slow road that most people take, if they take the road to authority status at all. What this really is… is an excuse, a logical explanation that we can lean on as to why expert status hasn't landed on us yet.

Most people think that in order to be considered an expert, they have to work years to build up their reputation by gaining more knowledge, doing that one more thing that will allow them to convince others that they are an expert at what they do. Then maybe, just maybe someone will come along and recognize them as an expert and then the media will even start talking about them.

It's a nice story they tell themselves. I'm sure it helps them feel that expert and authority status is coming, it's just down the road.

"Down the road." That's a dangerous thing to wait for. Especially since the reality is, you can position yourself in the media as an expert right now. You can let others see you as an authority because third party credible sources are already talking about you as that expert.

# Myth #5 – I'm not ready to step up as an authority right now.

One of the big obstacles that we see hard working entrepreneurs, unnecessarily, put in front of themselves is questioning their own authority.

"Am I really an authority? Am I really an expert? I don't know everything about everything in my industry; I'm just not comfortable calling myself an expert yet… but definitely DOWN THE ROAD."

Write this down, burn it into your brain:

IT'S NOT ABOUT CALLING YOUR SELF AN EXPERT!

Let's get this out of the way right now. Commit to yourself that you will never call yourself an expert again.

You also need to commit to yourself that you will freely allow others to call you the expert. Starting now.

Answer these questions. Don't hesitate or do them later. Don't read another word until you answer these two simple questions.

(1) Do you generally know more than your prospects about your industry, your product, or your service?

(2) Are you willing and able to help your prospects?

If you answered yes to these two questions then to us and many of your prospects you are an EXPERT.

Now that that's out of the way, let's bust the rest of these myths and show you why now is the time for you to step up and claim your authority.

# WHAT MAKES ME AN AUTHORITY?

We just told you why. You know more than your prospects and clients and you are able and willing to help them.

Think that's too easy? Let's examine some of the most popular business celebrities from different industries and figure out why they are considered experts. Why they are perceived to be authorities in their field?

If you look at people like Dave Ramsey, Suze Orman, Doctor Oz, Gary Vaynerchuk, and think about them and their authority positioning in their particular field. Are they the smartest in their fields? Are they the best at what they do in their field? Do they know everything about everything in their industry?

And now that you think about it, do they actually ever call themselves an expert? Do they refer to themselves as THE Authority?

How often do you see them yelling, "Buy my stuff. Buy my stuff."? Rarely if ever, right?

So why are they are perceived as authorities, even though they aren't doing any of the things that so many would have you think you need to do to be considered the expert?

They're not the smartest and they're not the best.

They don't call themselves the expert and they're not constantly yelling for you to buy their stuff.

Why? Perhaps it's because they happen to know more than their prospects and customers and they are able and willing to help them.

Wait a minute. What just happened? You want more? We have two words for you.

## **RICHARD SIMMONS**

Yes, Richard "Sweatin' To The Oldies" Simmons. He is a prime example that just demolishes these myths. Think about it.

Why do millions buy fitness advice from Richard Simmons?

Now, this isn't meant to be derogatory towards Richard Simmons. Quite the opposite in fact, he is actually the personification of how we define authority. Hold on, stick with us and you'll see what we mean.

If you ever feel the need to call yourself an expert, to think you have to be the best at what you do, or think you need to be better than your perceived competitors, just think about Richard Simmons. Is he the healthiest looking person? Is he more fit or more knowledgeable than other fitness gurus? I'm not even sure if that's debatable.

But what is definitely not debatable is the fact that Richard Simmons has built and empire by knowing more than his prospects and customers about getting healthier and he, without a doubt, is willing and able to help those that need it.

So ask yourself again, why is it that Richard Simmons, Suze Orman, Doctor Oz, Dave Ramsey, if they're not the best, if they are not the smartest and don't know everything about everything about their field, why are they the authorities? Why are they the expert celebrities in their fields?

There really is a simple answer. It's because they are Educators and Advocates for the success of their prospects and customers.

Read that once more, because it is probably the most important point and reason that you will be recognized as authority sooner rather than later.

Starting right now, go ahead and remove any fears, worries or pressure that you may have put on yourself to call yourself an expert or to convince others that you're the expert. Simply replace "I'm an expert" – with "I'm an educator and an advocate for the success of my customers and my prospects."

Do that and you'll see something remarkable happens. You'll immediately find yourself in the same position as the celebrity authorities in your field.

When you put yourself in the frame of mind of being the educator and the advocate for your customers' and your prospects' success, then you'll find that you never have to call yourself an expert again. Others will call you the expert.

And here's really the unfair reality when it comes to authority. When it comes to attracting new customers, it really doesn't matter if you have a degree. It doesn't matter how many products you purchased. It doesn't matter how many events you attended. It doesn't even matter how hard you work or how good you really are.

The truth is only one third of Americans say most people can be trusted. And if your prospects don't trust or believe or are convinced that you're an authority, you'll have to work ten times as hard to convert them into a customer.

However, if your prospects do trust that you're an authority, they see others looking at you as an authority, they see you being an educator and advocate for their success, then they'll pick you over your competition, even if it costs them more to work with you.

Perception is reality. Like it or not, our society has been conditioned to see the media as a credible source of information. They place their trust in the media. They're influenced by recommendations in the media. They give authority to those that are endorsed and seen in the media.

You know, Reader's Digest recently said that the four most trusted people in the world were Tom Hanks, Sandra Bullock, Denzel Washington and Meryl Streep. Well, they're no smarter or better than you are. In fact, you're probably brilliant compared to ninety-nine percent of the so-called experts featured in the media.

So that's really the simple formula. Getting media, third party people talking about you as that educator and advocate can create instant authority for you and your business.

**The Chicken or The Egg**

Remember the story about the chicken and the egg? Which came first? Do you want to wait and hope that media and third party credible sources might talk about you some day because you spent years calling yourself the expert?

Or would you rather have others see you as the expert right now because media and third party credible sources are talking about you today?

Well, it's possible. And it's actually easier and more accessible than you think. Becoming an authority and applying the secrets that the business gurus have been using to their advantage for years is something that you can do. But before you think about it, you really have to put yourself in that authority position.

And it's not about convincing your prospects or your clients that you're the expert. It's about convincing yourself that you are an authority.

It simply comes down to this. Can you look your prospects and customers in the eyes and say "I can help you".

And once you do that, that's when you truly become an authority and you can get paid like an authority.

*"The simple truth is if you aren't deliberately, systematically, methodically or rapidly and dramatically establishing yourself as a celebrity, at least to your clientele and target market, you're asleep at the wheel, ignoring what is fueling the entire economy around you, neglecting development of a measureable valuable asset."*

Dan Kennedy

# THE AUTHORITY MINDSET

Let's dig into what it means to be the Educator and Advocate for your prospects' and clients' success.

When a prospect feels that you understand them, provide valuable information, and they know you truly care about their results, then they see you as the expert… as their authority.

One of the misconceptions many entrepreneurs have that prevent moving towards authority status is, as a service provider, they put themselves in a servant position. Meaning they feel they need to offer anything and everything to serve their customer.

By doing that it can easily take them out of the role of the authority. When you attempt to serve a prospect by saying, "What would you like? What can I do? I can do anything for you. Tell me what you need me to do and I'll do it," – you have shifted from being an authority to being an order taker.

It's the difference between someone that is a landscape architect and someone that simply mows your grass and edges your lawn. The person that mows your grass and edges your lawn is someone that you give orders to to tell them what to do. "I want my grass mowed and I want the hedges trimmed and I want the edges."

But the landscape architect, you go to and say, "What

would you suggest? This is what I'm thinking but what can you do for my yard, for my landscaping?" Because that is an authority.

## Be The Doctor

Take a physician for example. The doctor is someone that you see as an authority. You see them as an expert. So put yourself in that position.

Think about when you go to the doctor. You don't get a menu of "Here's what I can do. I can pull out your tonsils. I can give you a shot. I can hit your knee with this hammer. Whatever you want me to do? I can do it."

What would you think? You'd be very concerned and your trust and confidence in that doctor would be very, very low.

You go to the doctor, not to give him or her instructions on what to do for you. You go to get their expert opinion, their advice on a solution to your problem.

That's the position you need to take. Think about the process. The doctor listens, and then the doctor diagnoses, then the doctor prescribes. That's what an educator and advocate does. The doctor doesn't say, "I think you should hire me to do this to you. I think you should pay me to do this. Here's my menu. I think you should order this."

What the doctor does is say, "Well, based on what you've told me, my suggestion would be that you do X, Y and Z." When you take that position, you're no longer the salesperson or that servant. You have just framed yourself as an educator and an advocate for their success. Because you've told them that you've listened to them, and based on their situation, offered a solution to their problem.

Yet you still haven't asked them to do business with you, but what you've just done is made them want to do business with you. Because now you're apples and oranges from anyone else. You've educated them. You're the advocate for their success. You have shown genuine concern for their outcome.

Even though you haven't asked them to do business, what naturally occurs more often than not is they respond with, "Is that something you can do? Is that something I can hire you to do?"

That's when you become the authority. When people try to hide or withhold information from their prospects, in fear that the prospect might want to do it themselves or not hire them, they are doing nothing more than diluting their authority positioning.

An authority is someone that will share. An authority is someone that will educate. An authority will be someone that will not withhold that information, because the truth is when someone sees you as an authority, they always feel that you have more. And they always feel that what you do is not a commodity. More importantly, it's not that they want to work with you because of your prices or your tools or your specific tactics.

They want to work with you because they want to work with you. Because you have shown them to be their educator and advocate and you are now the authority that they want to hire as their advisor.

So what's the difference between positioning yourself as an expert and positioning yourself as the educator and advocate?

We often find that when some are ready to be an authority, they feel that they have to do everything possible to convince others that they are the expert. How can I make them think that I'm the expert without calling myself an expert? What happens is they start making all their content about them rather than their prospects. They sound like a walking, talking resume.

We talked earlier that the real power of positioning yourself as an authority is not convincing people that you're the expert, but it's showing people that you are an educator and an advocate for their success.

This is when it is so vitally important that you make your marketing and your content about your prospects and customers and not about you. You must remind yourself to demonstrate your willingness and ability to share with them and have a genuine concern for their success. That's when they will resonate with you as the authority.

You really should write this down and keep it in front of you for some time until it is second nature.

**"I'm an educator and an advocate for the success**

**of my prospects and clients."**

When you approach content that you create from that mindset, when you create your marketing materials from that mindset, you automatically, and by default, make it about your customers.

One of the easiest exercises to do, one that we regularly do with our clients, is answer a simple question. If I was to meet you at a party or a networking event and asked, "What do you do?" – what would that reply sound like?

Almost 90 percent of the time, the reply begins with, "I am" or "I own." I am a chiropractor. I am a fitness instructor. I am a nutritionist. I am a real estate agent. I am a mortgage broker. Or I own XYZ company.

When you begin your reply with "I am" or "I own," you can bet on the rest of that conversation about you. That's where the momentum is going.

However, if you make a very purposeful effort and require yourself to begin that reply with "I help," then what you've just done is shifted the momentum to make the rest of that conversation about your prospects and your customers.

So in the case of a mortgage broker, rather than "I am a mortgage broker" or "I own a mortgage company," it begins with "I help first time home buyers." "I help homeowners reduce their mortgage debt". "I help..." You see how that works?

You've just made it all about your prospects and about their problems and the solutions that you can provide.

I would encourage you to take some time right now and craft that reply. It doesn't have to be perfect. You don't have to show it to anyone. But just so you see the difference in your own mind of what a difference it can make by being very deliberate about starting your reply with "I help" and speaking from the educator and advocate position – to make it about them, rather than yourself.

You'll quickly see how powerful it can be.

# THE FOUR FACES – YOUR AUTHORITY AVATAR

When people are looking to experts, the authority, what they really want is to be able to identify with leaders. They may want these leaders to have the attributes or the qualities that they want to achieve. They sometimes want the expert to have the attributes or qualities that they already recognize in themselves.

Think about that, a lot of people really do resonate and also admire people that have qualities that they recognize within themselves and they also have attributes or qualities that instill confidence in that authority's ability to solve their problem and that's one of the main and probably most important things that people look at when they start to follow that authority.

But what if they want their leader to possess qualities that they feel they could never achieve? Your Authority Avatar is something you should carefully consider before you make a big mistake in communicating with your prospects in a way that may actually push them away without you even knowing why?

This is why creating and developing your authority avatar...your authority persona is so important to your positioning and ability to connect with your prospects.

This doesn't mean you're going to create a completely different character from who you are. It's really going to be an extension of who you are naturally. As authentic as you can be, it's going to be easier for you to actually carry on those conversations at any given time and not have to go into your authority character.

You must be purposeful in the message and also in how you make people feel about you in the way that you create content and even the language that you use.

The base or core of your authority avatar is of course, the educator and advocate. You will build your persona on top of that.

There are four main categories that most people fall into when they are creating or developing this persona (avatar) and you will find that you will naturally fall into one of these four categories.

## We call these the Four Faces of Authority

1. Joe Everyman. This is the "If He or She Can Do It Then I Can Do It Too" authority persona.
2. The Cowboy. This is the No B.S. straight shooter authority persona.
3. The Soldier. This is the defender authority persona.

4. The Wizard. The magician avatar.

In the next section we will go deeper into each one of these so you can clearly identify and see which one you associate with. It really is a very natural process.

# JOE EVERYMAN

## IF THEY CAN DO IT, I CAN DO IT AUTHORITY

The Joe Everyman or If He or She Can Do It Then I Can Do It Too. People identify with this authority avatar as someone having a similar quality but also similar flaws as themselves. This authority is definitely not perfect and has battle scars from dealing with their own obstacles. People identify with this authority even with flaws because they've overcome something.

This authority cannot want to be the smartest person in the room. This is a very important point. We have seen this as being one of the biggest obstacles that several of our clients have had to overcome.

Many often feel that if they want to be seen as the expert they have to also be seen as the smartest person in the room. They have to be seen as having some kind of special intelligence or being extra clever or having some kind of special ability in order to be seen as the expert. What they find is that this can actually be very counterproductive and detrimental to the authority persona and hurt the connection and relationship with their prospects.

The power of the 'Joe Every Man' avatar is that they aren't so different from anyone else. They just happened to have discovered a way to succeed. Do you see how that may conflict with being the smartest person in the room?

The If He or She Can Do It Then I Can Do It Too attraction is based on the fact that this person found a path to success, whatever it may be, whether it was business, relationships, finance, or whatever. They found that path to success and now they're bringing back the map for others like them to be able to follow.

Jared from Subway is a great example of a person that was really overweight, obese, and he was just that guy that had flaws and issues like so many people, but he overcame them and that's why people looked to him as an inspiration, an authority, as someone to help guide them. People saw him as creating and developing the map or the path of losing weight by eating Subway sandwiches. He was bringing back the map to show them how they could do it as well.

The Joe Every Man Authority is very well suited for coaching. If you are a coach or selling info products or how-to information or systems, weight loss, fitness (of course) your audience would most likely connect with this persona. Think about some of the most successful fitness coaches. Many once had a really bad weight, health and fitness problem and then overcame that. That's why people resonate with them.... they see them as someone that overcame that and it helps them feel that they can do as well.

This can work with Business start-ups, money

management, people that see the authority as someone that's not much different than them with the same problems and same issues and challenges, but they were able to overcome them. That's a very powerful persona to have.

If you think about it, maybe that's the persona that you have. Maybe that's the persona that fits you as most aligned with your natural personality. However if it's not, or feels awkward, you probably don't want to force yourself into that avatar.

# FOUR FACES OF AUTHORITY

FOUR FACES OF AUTHORITY

# THE COWBOY

## NO BS AUTHORITY

The Cowboy authority persona can be very compelling because it often makes people uncomfortable. Making others uncomfortable with this No B.S. avatar isn't a bad thing and can be quite a powerful position when your audience is likely to connect with someone who is tough, firm, but still compassionate.

You can probably think of some Cowboy business celebrities in your industry right now. The No B.S. authority strengthens prospects' trust by concurring with their hesitations and their doubts but then giving them rational and realistic solutions.

Let's use weight loss again. The Cowboys are the ones saying: "Of course you haven't lost weight. Of course you lose weight and then you gain it back. Of course you do because it's hard to have will power and hard to not eat the stuff you want." They're saying stuff that goes against what they've heard before. If others say it's easy then the Cowboy, No B.S. persona is saying: "Well, of course they say it's easy, but it isn't easy, but there is a way."

Then they give a rational realistic solution to how the real way, the logical way that it can work.

This avatar may or may not be the smartest person in the room, but the one thing is that they have the guts to say what everyone else is thinking. You think about celebrity Cowboy authorities like Jim Cramer, Gary Vaynerchuk or Larry Winget.

These No B.S. personas are very bold and brash and tell it like it is. There's usually no spoon full of sugar to help the medicine go down.

Prospects that resonate with this avatar may feel like they lack discipline to succeed because they've always fallen for easy answers. They want someone who's going to whip them into shape.

This works well in fitness and nutrition and is why people hire personal trainers that are going to push them further than they could push themselves. They want accountability.

The Cowboy avatar works well with how-to products. I'm sure you've heard " The No B.S. way to X, Y, & Z."

People want a No. B.S. coach that's going to tell them when they're wrong. They're not going to be yes men. They're going to give them the real straight answers.

Chances are if this your persona you recognized it early in this section. Remember it's not about creating a new personality it's an extension of who you are naturally.

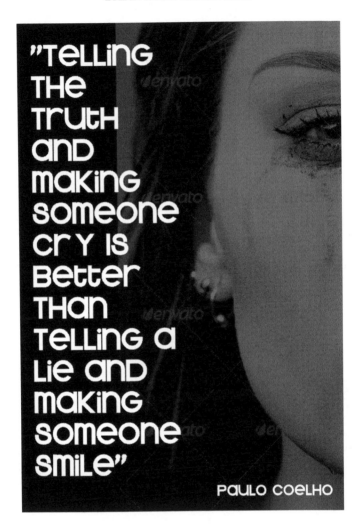

# THE SOLDIER

## DEFENDER AUTHORITY

The Soldier is an authority avatar that can be extremely effective especially when it is very tightly aligned with your natural authentic self because the soldier is someone that has knowledge, the willingness and the ability to make problems go away. They are a natural defender. They can make good things happen. They can steer prospects and customers in the right direction while avoiding pitfalls.

The Soldier can instill confidence and is sometimes perceived as the smartest person in the room, and that's okay. Think about celebrity experts like Dave Ramsey or Suze Orman. The customers or the prospects that feel overwhelmed or defenseless are the types of prospects that connect with this defender.

This avatar works well in health and wellness, legal, financial. Think about consumer advocates. These are people that are coming to your defense. Perhaps an attorney, especially if they help people defend against the IRS, they are going to help the underdog. They say, "There is a solution, and it's not your fault that you don't know what it is."

This works well in a lot of different areas.

Finance, alternative medicine, legal specialties. Anywhere that prospects and customers feel like

David against Goliath.

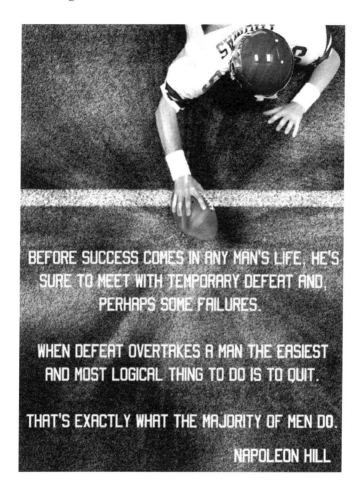

FOUR FACES OF AUTHORITY

# THE WIZARD

Now the Wizard is a persona that few actually should take on, but so many mistakenly feel they need to have prospects and customers perceive them as the smartest person in the room. The Wizard has specialized knowledge and powers. The Wizard can do things that the average person cannot do.

The Wizard avatar connects very strongly with customers and prospects that can benefit just by being part of this wizard's world - just by being around them or allowing them to work their magic on the prospect's problem. The Wizard is often perceived as the smartest or most gifted person in the room.

If you think about Wizard avatars or personas, think about people like Tony Robbins, innovators like Steve Jobs, or inspirational speakers like Joel Olsteen. These are personalities that have achieved a level of authority and produce results that your average person wouldn't feel they could attain themselves.

They feel that they benefit by being part of that wizard's world. They benefit by being surrounded by that wizard's energy or knowledge and that can be very alluring to a lot of people when developing their authority avatar. They want to be seen as that wizard, but it can backfire it doesn't match up with your prospects.

The Wizard works really well with people that are inspirational speakers, consultants, or medical specialists. Prospects resonate with this avatar just by being in the presence of their people by letting them do their thing, work their magic on the problem. They are considered to have some sort of special knowledge, skill or gift.

# WHICH AUTHORITY ARE YOU?

So which authority are you? What is the product or solution you provide? Is it coaching, consulting, information, how-to products? Is it Done For You services, physical products? Let's look at some examples.

Coaching – If you're a coach, chances are you're going to be okay being the Joe Every Man, Cowboy or Soldier.

The Wizard, however, can present challenges because if your prospects feel that you have some kind of special gift or special talent, or an advantage to gaining your position, they may not feel that they achieve those results. They may feel like "Oh, well, that's why he or she is successful. I'll never... I don't have that so it won't work for me." You have to be extremely careful about that.

Consulting – You've got to be careful about taking on the Joe Every Man avatar here. If you're a consultant and people are hiring you to come in and do things for them or implement systems do you really want them to feel that you're the person that... "Well, gosh, if this person can do this there's no reason we can't do it."

You can certainly be the Cowboy. You can be the Soldier. You can even be the Wizard. Those work really well for consulting because people want

consultants to have some special talent or some special knowledge that they don't have or could easily attain. They usually don't want to know how it works, they just want the consultant to make it work.
If you're selling information, how-to products or training the Joe Every Man is certainly a great avatar. You want your prospects to feel very much that they can do it.

The No B.S. Cowboy avatar who cuts to the chase and shows you exactly how it's done works nicely as well. Soldier can work in this area, but a lot of times people see the Soldier as that defender that's going to be with them each step. That the Soldier will be there giving them strength or to help them past the obstacles that they feel they can't get past on their own.

Now if the information is able to do that then that would work fine, but it has to be positioned correctly.

The Wizard can be tough as well. People may find that they won't have the ability to implement wizard information if it's a how-to type product. For example, the Queen of England would not do well selling information on "How To Be The Queen of England" because most people realize that there's no amount of information that will allow them to achieve that. They're not going to be the Queen of England no matter how hard they try or how much knowledge they acquire.

Done For You Services – Joe Every Man can work sometimes. It really depends on what you are providing. Services like changing oil, mowing lawns. These might be services you would pay someone to do even though you could certainly do them if you wanted to, but you may not want to. The problem is it rarely works with high value services.

The Cowboy and the Soldier works well. Even the Wizard avatar works for services...anything that's done for you.

What about combining two avatars? We have clients often say "you know, I kind of see myself as a crossover between the Joe Every Man and the Cowboy." That's ok. You may have attributes of a combination of these that can easily blend together if it fits with the audience and prospects that you are working with; however, we have never ever seen a situation where the combination of Joe Every Man and the Wizard has worked.

This is something we would recommend that you never ever try to combine. We have seen it really be the downfall of some really talented entrepreneurs because they didn't recognize hazardous position they had put themselves in. It really comes to, for lack of a better term, self-esteem.

Entrepreneurs thinking that if they're going to be seen as an authority or an expert that they have to be seen as the smartest person in the room. The combination of Joe Everyman and the Wizard does not mix.

When people resonate with the If He or She Can Do It Then I Can Do Too, if they want to feel that that person has the same flaws, the same challenges, and overcame the same types of obstacles that they overcame, they will immediately lose that connection if they feel that authority had a special talent or gift, or were given a privileged situation in order to make that happen. It just doesn't work.

So be very careful about feeling like you need to be the smartest person in the room or imply that you have some special advantage if your audience really needs the Joe Every Man.

# DON'T TRY AND PLEASE EVERYONE

Here's something else to watch out for: the strong pull to try and please everyone. Generally you're going to lose. Being seen as an Authority can require some degree of personality that will polarize. What does that mean? Not everyone will resonate with you. Not everyone's going to like you. Not everyone can like you if you're going to be successful.

Think about Rush Limbaugh or Howard Stern. 90% of the population does not connect or even like these personalities. In fact, a lot of them passionately dislike them.

If an authority tries to appeal to the preferences of everyone then no one is going to be passionate about their message. You want to try to lean to the extreme to a certain extent. You don't have to go all the way to the extreme, but you want to lean to the extreme to work with a very specialized group of folks that will really resonate with you.

There's a rule of thirds that the automobile industry uses. The most popular cars are generally designed so that they would cause a third of the consumers to absolutely hate it, a third of the consumers to absolutely love it, and then the remaining third is indifferent or isn't really paying attention.

Why is that? If you think about it the most expensive cars are built to appeal to the passion of a minority of consumers. If a car is built to avoid the dislikes of the majority of people, no one is going to be really passionate about driving that car, and that's really something that they're going to have to compete on price. If you try to just blend in and not offend anyone, you have really no choice but to compete in price. You'll have very few enthusiasts out there for your product or your service. Then you commoditize yourself and it really does come down to which one is cheaper. There's no real drive or passion around what you're saying to your audience, the people that follow you, the people are going to call you the authority.

It's rare that anyone is going to call someone an authority that doesn't take a position and really focus on that position. Which authority are you?

Always remember your core is being the educator and advocate for your prospects' and customers' success.

If you frame your positioning as being the educator and advocate for the success of your prospects and your customers it really is tough to mess it up. Figure out what resonates with you and chances are it's going to be a very natural choice. So what we'd like to encourage you to do is commit to which authority you are going to be and get busy being it.

# CLAIMING YOUR AUTHORITY

Now that you know the secrets and power of creating your Authority Avatar with intention and by design, you should also know how so many national business celebrities and industry leaders created that spark that started the kindling and eventually grew into a blaze of attention and recognition as the Authority in their field.

Have you noticed how the national media highlights certain people in their stories as experts and leaders, positions them as authorities, and even celebrity status?

...even when you know there are far more qualified people in that field? You probably know just as much or more than some of the recognized experts in your field.

But here's the thing...

Having online media coverage seems like luck or being at the right place at the right time, right? But it rarely is.

In fact, there is a easy way for you to be positioned as an authority in digital media and on national news and business websites. The "secret sauce" is simply a bone-deep understanding of human psychology that veteran entrepreneurs have used for years.

Every single one of them knows a certain truth that less than half of a percent of their competition takes advantage of.

It's not magic, luck, or rocket science. However it is essential to getting the upper hand on your competition, and putting yourself in the driver's seat for instant recognition as the Authority in your field.

Once you understand the science behind this method, the sky's the limit...

The truth is, filling your appointment book is much easier, and selling your products and services, happens quicker--when OTHERS talk about you. Especially in trusted national media outlets.

We've created a unique way to make our clients stars in their audience's eyes, build quick "bridges" for them to increased trust and likability, and install almost overnight credibility in their marketing messages.

**Our results speak for themselves.** These publicity tactics are seldom seen by your peers simply because it SEEMS so difficult to do.

Think about this and it will make complete sense to you to move forward with me.

- **Your audience sees that the media** takes notice of you, and instantly YOU become more credible, more trustworthy and they are therefore more eager to turn to you for advice.
- **You get celebrity and an "insider"** status in your audience's eyes that you can turn off and on at will.
- **You'll get the satisfaction that you and your business is MILES ahead of any competition.** This allows every dollar you spend in advertising to be more effective

Think about how your prospect would view you when they see you are featured as an industry expert on radio shows and podcasts, national online news and business websites and magazines, even written about and quoted as an industry Authority on sites like CNN, Yahoo News and dozens of ABC, NBC, CBS, FOX affiliates.

Who is going to be seen as more credible? You are!

And those who turn to you for advice are far more likely to buy. Every time you step up to the plate. Not necessarily because of your fancy words or phrases in your ads, although that matters deeply...

But simply because other, third party, credible and trusted resources have recognized you as the expert on your subject. And then they've gone and **FEATURED** you as the Authority.

# AUTHORITY ALCHEMY

**al-che-my:** The power or process of turning something ordinary into something very special

That's what we do every single week for our Authority Alchemy clients and it's what we can do for you.

Are you ready to claim your Authority and be recognized as the expert in your industry in the next 48 hours?

Visit http://authorityalchemy.com/ready to learn how.

We would love to work with you.

## About Jack and Brian

Jack Mize and Brian Horn are the pioneers of "authority marketing" and hosts of the top ranked marketing podcast, Authority Alchemy (AuthorityAlchemy.com).

Jack Mize is a speaker, best selling author, trainer and one of the most respected and sought after Online Media Marketing Strategists for small business owners and and local marketing consultants.

Brian Horn is long time entrepreneur, best selling author, speaker and contributor to The Huffington Post on the topic of "authority marketing".

Together, they help business owners, executives and service professionals to position themselves as the Educator and Advocate for their prospects' and customers' success.

They find magic in each of their clients, help them position it, get national media attention, then leverage that attention into more customers and profits.

# GARRET J WHITE ON
AUTHORITY ALCHEMY

Hello, my friends. This is Garrett J. White, the Master Coach Mentor and Leader of the Wake Up Warrior movement and a client of Authority Alchemy.

I signed up for the Authority Alchemy Number One Best Seller Campaign. I signed up for the Positioning with Press Releases, etc. and the one thing I can tell you is simply this.

See, you're going to spend a lot of time in your marketplace becoming an expert at what you do. And I can tell you that becoming the expert is not the same as being positioned as the expert in your marketplace.

I can't tell you how many years of frustration I went through in business, knowing my value, feeling my value, wanting the marketplace to see my value, and then with one subtle shift, it changed literally over about a month time period.

And what it came down to is, all of a sudden, I'm a Number One Best Seller. All of a sudden, I've got press releases in the Wall Street Journal. "As Seen On" CNN, NBC, Fox and affiliates, etc. And all of a sudden, things I was saying before, a whole group of people now are taking more seriously.

What I learned from this process is when you invest your money into positioning who you are, positioning your brand and positioning your offer to the marketplace, you create for yourself results that otherwise the marketplace can't ever perceive.

See, particularly online, around the globe for worldwide-based businesses like mine, where my marketplace reaches into world-based economies, dealing with clients all over the world through my online marketing systems and offers with the Wake Up Warrior Movement, the thing I can tell is at the end of the day, all that's left for the consumer in their mind is two things: number one, the offers that you're making, and number two, the positioning of the offers that you're making.

Now, if you're looking for a guaranteed system, a guaranteed way to take what you currently offer and to package it and position it in a way that allows other people to see its value, well, then Authority Alchemy is the answer.

If you're looking for some lucky-ass home run out of nowhere and you deliver shit on a stick and your stuff sucks, guess what? I would tell you to stay far away.

But if you're somebody that has a legitimate business,

a legitimate offer and makes a legitimate different in the marketplace, you owe it to yourself, you owe it to your clients, you owe it to your family to invest time, energy and money in Authority Alchemy and get yourself positioned correctly.

Two major things will happen when you do this. Number one, the perception of the marketplace will change in what they see in you.

Secondly, these little tags and this experience of feeling your brand accelerate through Authority Alchemy will also change the way you see yourself.

And honestly, at the end of the day, that's the most important piece, is how do you change the perception of lesser value to higher value in yourself and how do you shift the perception of lesser value to higher value in the marketplace?

Well, I'm going to consider that one of the things that you're going to do is sign up for the Authority Alchemy process. Get yourself in a number one best seller list. Get yourself positioned.

This, itself, has exploded my business in a way that I can't describe, except for Big-Ass Results. Big-Ass Positioning. And a movement that ultimately I felt called to lead forever, finally in the last twelve to fourteen months exploded the way deep in my soul I always knew was possible.

So if you're a Warrior trying to wake up and you've got a business and you're trying to get the world to wake up to hear your product, service and experience offering, don't be stupid. Invest the time, energy and money in Authority Alchemy today.

Thanks so much.

This is Garrett J. White reminding you the power in today's marketplace as the modern-day warrior comes down to the simple formula of authenticity.

Be Real. Get Raw. And Stay Relevant, with a ruthless commitment to creating Big-Ass Results today.

Garret J White – WakeUpWarrior.com

Printed in Poland
by Amazon Fulfillment
Poland Sp. z o.o., Wrocław